BE THE SUN

NOT THE SALT

by Dr. Harry D. Cohen

Dedication

To Jan, Ethan, Jeremy and Yolo.
There is no doubt that each one of us won the lottery
to have each other as our family. You guys are my sun.

FOREWORD

Several years ago, a colleague told me about a man he'd met through some leadership training sessions at Ford Motor Company. He had a Ph. D. in Psychology from the University of Michigan and my colleague suggested that he could do some executive coaching for our company's leaders, providing them with training that would help their employees grow as individuals and work together better as teams. I was open to the idea, but I also wondered…do we really need a corporate shrink?

My first encounter with Harry did not bode well. He came to speak to a group of managers and, for the life of him, could not remember my name. When I raised my hand to answer a question, he'd outstretch his arm and waggle his fingers in my face with an "uh…uh…" as if this motion would trigger his memory. I got even by calling him "Henry." But as he continued to speak I noticed that the managers around me were really engaged, physically leaning into the conversation, nodding often at the points he made. There was something going on here.

In a short time, Harry went from someone on the agenda at a training meeting to an integral part of our team. He currently spends two weeks a month meeting one-on-one with our key people across the country. He recently spent three full days with a team of business leaders away on a semi-annual retreat.

When our board of directors held a months' long formal Strategic Planning initiative, Harry was in the room. For our business, we trust him with our plans and priorities; as individuals, we trust him with our foibles and fears.

I've noticed that even when Harry is absent, he is present; many of my colleagues have added Harry-isms to their lexicon. When someone is caught doing something especially well, I'll hear, "Do more of THAT, please." We talk about "camping" with our people, Harry's term for those precious conversations that are not about productivity or performance but about a father's recent illness or a daughter's latest dance recital. Our CEO often espouses his goal of becoming "an Olympic listener." We remind each other that people might not remember what you said but they'll remember how you made them feel. And when there is a heartbeat of a moment when I can choose how to respond to a situation, a voice in my head says, "Be the sun, not the salt." Harry is part of the fabric of our company and our lives.

You'll find that Harry's teachings are straightforward and simple, and that is part of their beauty. But what makes them truly special is that they come from a place of goodness, a place of forgiveness, a place of love. What you'll discover in the coming pages is not rocket science. But if most of us could abide by his principles ("Smile." "Apologize well." "Don't be a jerk.") imagine — I mean, really imagine — how different our world would be. You're likely to read ahead and think, "Yeah, yeah, yeah…I know this stuff." But there is a huge difference between knowing and doing. I challenge you to do.

I thought, those many years ago, that we were hiring a corporate shrink, and I guess that's how it started out. But what I have now is a treasured friend and confidant to whom I entrust the full of my trepidations and my joys. His wisdom has made me a better leader and a better person. Read on, take action, and he can do that for you, too.

Melinda (Mindy) K. Holman
Chairman of the Board, Holman Enterprises, Inc.

INTRODUCTION

The heliotropic effect is the tendency for all living systems to be drawn to energy that sustains its life. Like gravity, the heliotropic effect is a powerful, invisible force that we can harness if we understand it. Just as a plant on the windowsill tilts towards the sun, we are attracted and drawn to people who express those qualities that energize us. We call these people positive energizers.

Conversely, we recoil from people who deplete us. Negative people who make critical remarks are like salt on the roots of a plant.

So, Be the Sun, Not the Salt.

This book is intended to be helpful. Each chapter is purposefully brief. I've tried to say as much as I can with as few words as possible. If one concept doesn't grab you, move on to the next. Each of these bits have proven to be helpful to someone.

Why should you read this book?
Put even the smallest effort behind any of these ideas and you will be more successful and fulfilled no matter what your life circumstances. Here's the cool part: with deliberate practice, it gets easier and easier to live in the world as a positive energizer.

Acknowledgments

For the past decade or so, the Holman Family has allowed me to be part of the lives of so many of their people. I'm honored and humbled by how much those relationships have taught me as I tried my best to be of service to them. They have created a company that at its core truly wants the best for and from its people. Everyone from the receptionist to the CEO show people that they care. As I try to explain to others how special they are, I fail every time. I'm not giving up.

A special thanks to Dr. Kim Cameron, a professor from the University of Michigan Ross School of Business, who first wrote and spoke about the heliotropic effect and its effect on leaders and organizations.

There are hundreds of Ford dealers and former and current executives who have contributed to the articulation of this collection of helpful ideas. I would like to call these ideas wisdom but perhaps that's too presumptuous. There are too many people to thank, but hopefully they will see their contributions in these pages.

One of those Ford executives invited me to a retreat years ago where I was inspired by a group of people who were already doing seriously massive good in the world. I had to overcome this silly thought: "I am not worthy." Thank you, Bob Chapman,

Simon Sinek, Bill Uhry, Scott Harrison, Gary Slutkin, Charles Kim. You guys planted a seed, the TEDx talk was a sprout and I hope this idea spreads like a healthy virus.

I also want to thank my dear friends whose continued support and continued edits and suggestions just kept making it "more and more better." Bobby, Doug, Dick and Steve, thank you.

My sister Patty is going to love getting mentioned here. She deserves it. As a positive cancer thriver, she embodies a perfect example of every one of us who's trying her best to be a little bit better, even though she's already quite wonderful.

There is no way I could do this without the help of the team that Connie put together: Mary Kae, Linda and Lauren. It's one thing to write down some ideas, it's quite another to illustrate and package it so people can digest and metabolize it easily.

Finally, to the thousands of customers who've enjoyed the Black Pearl and the hundreds of employees who have worked there, thank you for allowing us to practice creating an environment where people feel the sun and hopefully not the salt.

Table of Contents

Table of Contents

Do the Next Right Thing

Pet Peeves Bite

Knowing Isn't Doing

01 DO ALL THE GOOD YOU CAN

When I speak about the heliotropic effect, I am talking about the idea of doing all the good you can. As often as you can. Wherever you can. There is no downside to being kind and no drawbacks to making situations better. Actually, you are likely to find that you feel more fulfilled when you think and act in a heliotropic manner.

People will be drawn to you and want to be around you.

You will be more effective in every role you play.

You will feel good immediately.

And the great news is, the more you practice it, the more automatic it becomes. Like the sun, people who act in heliotropic ways can create a dramatic impact on their environment. Anyone can do it. Yes, anyone.

Anyone can do it.
Yes, anyone.

02 BE HELPFUL

It doesn't matter what circumstances we find ourselves in, there is a good chance we can find a way to be helpful in some way, shape or form. We always have choices.

You and I can either make something better, or worse. Or neither.

> ## BEFORE YOU SPEAK, ASK YOURSELF IF IT WILL BE HELPFUL.

If you can help, do so. If not, say nothing. Do nothing. The Hippocratic Oath that all doctors ascribe to is: First, do no harm. This is true for all of us.

Before you speak, ask yourself if it will be helpful.

How can you be helpful?

You can be helpful if you express your point of view with an understanding that your approach may not be the one "right" way but simply another option to consider.

You can be helpful if you explain something simply. Clear communication promotes fuller understanding and better outcomes.

You can be helpful if you prevent something unwise from happening. Contributing a fresh perspective in a shaky situation might help someone arrive at a more thoughtful decision.

You can be helpful if you make something better (and even more helpful if you don't make something worse).

You can be helpful if you make someone laugh. It may be just what she needs at that moment to help her move forward.

Whatever words we utter should be chosen with care, for people will hear them and be influenced by them for good or ill.
– Buddha

03 RESPECT PEOPLE'S FEELINGS

A client told me that one of the most helpful things that
I suggested was to think about the way he makes people feel.
He said he now thinks about it whenever anyone leaves his office.

Yes, we can make other people feel things. Hope, fear, confusion,
excitement, enthusiasm, confidence, anger, disappointment,
anxiety. What we say and do can affect the way that people feel
in any given moment. So, it's important that you pay attention
and respect the feelings of others.

Think about your intention when you interact with people.
What is the feeling that you would like to leave them with?
This is the essence of being the sun and not the salt.

Do you want to make them feel like you're pouring sun on their
leaves? Or salt on their roots?

If you aren't sure how someone is feeling about what you say or
do, look at the expression on her face. Or better yet, take out
the guesswork and ask her.

SMILE AT A STRANGER
AND SEE WHAT HAPPENS.

By the way, you don't have to be a leader of a company to have an impact on people. You don't even have to know a person to make him feel something. Just smile at a stranger and see what happens.

 I've learned that people will forget what you said, people will forget what you did, but people will never forget how you made them feel.
– Maya Angelou

04 SHOW YOU CARE

Another client summed up the culture that earned her company a spot on *Fortune* magazine's Best Place to Work list. "We care. That's it, but it's a lot."

Someone else I know refers to it as, "Authentic give a $%!#." Whatever you call it, having empathy, understanding and showing you care can make a real difference. People feel your emotional response immediately and appreciate it.

Think about it. Let's say you are at the airport and your flight is canceled. When you approach the ticket agent, she treats you with genuine compassion, saying "I'm truly sorry for the hassle; let me try my best to get you on another flight." She did not change the fact that your flight was canceled, but she probably helped you feel less agitated and reduced anxiety by helping you with the next step.

That's what showing you care means. Acting on your words. Following up. Doing something that makes a difference for someone. What if you really don't care? Well, my advice is don't pretend that you do. Nobody can fake caring. You won't fool anyone.

> ## CARING IS A LEARNABLE SKILL.

What if you don't care but would like to? Good news! Caring is a learnable skill. All you have to do is put yourself in the other person's situation, think about how you would feel and treat him or her accordingly.

Nobody cares how much you know,
until they know how much you care.
— Theodore Roosevelt

05 BE YOUR BEST SELF

My coaching philosophy can be summarized by four words:
Do more of that!

When you are at your best, what does it look like?
Do more of THAT!

How does your best self act? It's simple observation.
If you were at your best self just this morning — how did you act?

Chances are you were patient, kind, thoughtful, prepared or showed any number of positive attributes.

No, you were not perfect. (Just so you know, no one is perfect, so take that pressure off yourself.)

Ask someone you trust what you do when you're at your best. Listen to what they say. Take it in. Do it again.

This, by the way, is not about learning to be someone else. Being heliotropic is about being yourself, the self-that-uplifts-others' version of yourself. Your best self.

Do More of That.

ople who are heliotropic reveals a common
.ors.

He.   ic people:
Smile.
Keep their word.
Are kind, dependable, honest.
Do the hard work.
Listen well.
Speak thoughtfully.
Are compassionate, forgiving, curious and mindful of others.

> # HELIOTROPIC PEOPLE WANT
> # THE BEST FOR OTHERS.

No one is perfect at all times. But intention matters. Heliotropic people strive to be better than they are. To improve. To grow. To be their best selves. Heliotropic people want the best for others, so they make a point to pour sun on other people's leaves.

Pouring sun on people's leaves may come in the form of a genuine smile that makes someone feel good, honesty that creates a trusted friendship, or a thoughtful comment that helps someone move forward.

Example isn't the main thing in influencing others. It is the only thing.
– Albert Schweitzer

07 APOLOGIZE WELL

Apologizing is a very simple skill that people should learn early in life. In case you haven't, take a moment to learn now. Making a genuine apology is as simple as expressing honest regret for doing something that had a negative effect on someone else. That's it. No more, no less.

A genuine apology begins with the words, "I am sorry," and is followed by a statement that takes responsibility for an action. When you apologize, do it in a way that demonstrates that you feel bad about causing another person to suffer. Make it clear that you didn't mean to and that you will make every effort not to do it again.

> # MAKING A GENUINE APOLOGY IS AS SIMPLE AS EXPRESSING HONEST REGRET.

Fake apologies, on the other hand, are transparent — people see right through them. And are, therefore, salt on their roots.

Examples of poor apologies:

"I'm sorry you got upset."
This apology does not take responsibility for
the action that caused the upset.

"For whatever I did, I'm sorry."
This apology is vague. The person apologizing does not care enough to find out what he or she did.

"I'm sorry, but..."
Sounds, and most-likely is, insincere.

"I'm sorry, I can't help it."
Really? Chances are pretty good that one can help it.

Examples of good apologies:

"I'm truly sorry I was short with you; I have no excuse. I will be careful not to do that to you again."

"Forgive me; it is not my intention to be rude to you, ever!"

It's also a good idea to remove the word "just" from an apology as in, "I was just trying to..." It's a word that tends to minimize an action rather than take responsibility for it.

What's better than being good at apologizing? Curtailing certain behaviors. Think before you speak or act. Don't interrupt. Don't be rude. Considered actions rarely need apologies.

POSITIVE INTENT

.ious, inadvertent and unintentional are three words that ιcredibly helpful. All of us occasionally do things that are ιscious, inadvertent or unintentional.

Although we strive to be deliberate and direct, we sometimes screw up. When you screw up, own up to it right away and apologize well.

> _"Oh, excuse me, I wasn't paying attention.
> You were next in line; please go ahead."_

> _"I'm sorry I took your chair; I didn't realize
> you were sitting here."_

> _"It wasn't my intention to make you feel excluded,
> but I understand how you'd feel that way. I'm sorry."_

You meant well, but you are human; you made a mistake. And that is my point when I say to assume the best. Assume positive intent by others until proven otherwise. Cut other people the same slack that you'd like them to cut you, because they, too, make mistakes that are unconscious, inadvertent and unintentional.

> # CUT OTHER PEOPLE THE SAME SLACK
> # THAT YOU'D LIKE THEM TO CUT YOU.

One more thing. Don't walk around with a clipboard like you are in charge of everyone's proper conduct. For one thing, it will exhaust all those around you. For another, it's salt-on-roots behavior.

Instead, practice seeing conduct that you perceive as bad as being done by people in a momentary lapse in judgment and not as proof that they are bad. If you can get there, it's a nice place to be. For you and everyone else.

09 WIN-WIN ALWAYS WINS

A friend shared the notion of helping everyone win, and I've cherished it ever since. Learning to think in terms of win-win solutions is very heliotropic. By win-win I mean that in any deal where two people are trying to work something out, no one ends up feeling ripped off. It's the mutual understanding that nothing is settled until both people are satisfied with the outcome.

Think about it. If you know that a person has an attitude of fairness, you feel pretty good dealing with that person.

On the other hand, if you think someone is completely comfortable getting the better end of the stick all of the time — one for you, two for me — you are likely to feel crappy or defensive, even before you start talking.

This is true in business, marriage and in all relationships. How on earth can you be in a partnership if one side is comfortable with the other side getting less? It's unfair. It's win-lose. And it's definitely not good for the long-term health of the partnership.

> WHEN ONE PLANT BLOCKS
> ANOTHER FROM THE SUN,
> THE PLANT IN THE SHADOW
> DOES NOT GROW AS WELL, IF AT ALL.

To put it in terms of the heliotropic metaphor, when one plant blocks another from the sun, the plant in the shadow does not grow as well, if at all.

So, don't overthink this. If something feels one-sided, find a solution that works for both sides. If you can't, understand that the relationship will eventually fail.

10 Don't hang with cilantro

Some of the most powerful advice that I have been given is to:

Be good company
and keep good company.

A simple way to live heliotropically is to surround yourself with people who make you feel good about you. They are the sun on your leaves.

A friend shared the counsel he gave his son who was dealing with a relationship issue. He told his son to ask himself, *"How do I feel about myself when I am with this person?"* The answer is a good gauge in judging whether a person is good company for you, or not.

> SURROUND YOURSELF WITH PEOPLE
> WHO BRIGHTEN YOUR OUTLOOK.

I am not talking about hanging with people who puff up your ego or flatter you. I am encouraging you to surround yourself with people who brighten your outlook. Who nourish you. Who make you want to be your best self. These are probably the same people with whom you feel safe enough to show your true self.

Striving to be good company means that you are good for the people you're with. The easiest way to be good company is to be a good friend. Chances are you already know how to do that.

Being good company is a noble pursuit, and trying to avoid bad company is good, too. But, as you know, nobody is perfect. Sometimes it takes a while to get it right.

If you eat something that doesn't agree with you, hopefully, you learn not to eat it again. Some people have a gene that makes cilantro taste like soap. If people are like cilantro for you, don't hang out with them.

Listen to your body: "How do I feel when I'm with this person?" If being with certain people makes you feel good, spend more time with them. If not, don't.

11 LEARN TO WALK AWAY

I talked about keeping good company, but what about those times when you don't have complete control over your situation? When you spend your days with unpleasant coworkers? Or relatives who bring out the worst in you? People who make you feel like crap because they are mean, unaware, phony, petty, cynical, arrogant, self-righteous? I am sure you have your own list of attributes that you assign to people who make your roots want to shrivel right up.

The reality is that there are times when you have to put up with less-than-ideal situations. For instance, your boss is a jerk, but you need the job. Remind yourself that in the moment, saying nothing is in your best interest. But also remember that you have power. In the case of a bad boss, challenge yourself to find a new job. A better situation. Unpleasant coworkers? Don't acknowledge complaints or bad behavior. If you ignore their behavior, they are likely to move on to someone else.

A salty relative? You have more power than you think. You may have to learn to disengage emotionally and refuse to participate in anyone else's drama. It may drive them crazy, but it will keep you sane. In the same vein, if someone is smoking and you don't like it, move. If someone at a party is full of nasty gossip, go refresh your drink.

> BE GRACEFUL. BE KIND.
> AND WHEN YOU FIND YOURSELF IN THE
> PRESENCE OF SALT, BE GONE.

Don't overthink. Don't complain. Don't lament. Decide what the best action is and take it. Remember, being heliotropic means protecting your roots. Be graceful. Be kind. And when you find yourself in the presence of salt, be gone. It will take thought. It will take effort. But it can be done. Practice courage, compassion and forgiveness, and learn to walk away.

 HOLD THE SALT

For some people, being the sun is a bridge too far. Some days
it's just too far for any of us; we all have those moments.
When you are in that place, just know that it's still really powerful
to not pour salt on people's roots.

Bite your tongue. You don't need to say everything you think.
Refraining from raining on people's parades is so obvious that it
may seem ridiculous to bring it up. But sometimes reminders
are good.

Just as there are so many ways to be heliotropic, there are
as many ways to be the salt. Don't be!

Don't be a talking machine. Stop. Listen.

Don't be a jerk. Observe your behavior and turn it around.

Don't be a drag to be around. Loosen up. Brighten up.
Make it your aim to inspire.

Don't be a fault-finder or blame-thrower.
If there is a problem, help solve it.

> ## BITE YOUR TONGUE. YOU DON'T NEED TO SAY EVERYTHING YOU THINK.

It's a lot easier to see when other people are being jerks than when we are. But if you take care to become aware, you will begin to notice when you pour salt on someone's roots. When you observe that it happened, you have a choice: you can do it again, or not.

You don't have to complicate it, just make a correction. Don't interrupt next time. Stop yourself from assigning blame.

Now, if you don't care about pouring salt on other people's roots, well, maybe this book can't help you. Still, you could do something kind in the moment. Give this book to someone else. Giving a gift is a heliotropic thing to do.

13 BE YOUR OWN BEST FRIEND

The concept of being your own best friend can also be thought of as protecting your own roots — from yourself. I am talking about negative self-talk, our critical inner dialogue, the nasty things that we often think about ourselves.

The first thing to do is to pay attention to the negative thoughts you have about yourself. And, once you become aware, begin to challenge them. Right after you say some version of

> *"I can't believe I did that, I'm such a jerk,"*

turn it around and say,

> *"Actually, I am not a jerk. I made a mistake and I'll try not to do that again."*

In other words, show yourself some compassion. Continually challenge your negative self-talk. Like our bodies, our minds are creatures of habit. Pouring salt on our own roots is merely a bad mental habit. That's it! Putting ourselves down is a bad habit, nothing more.

Fortunately, with a little work and a little self-kindness, this habit can be broken. Work towards being your own best friend. You are worth the effort.

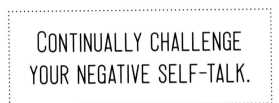

CONTINUALLY CHALLENGE YOUR NEGATIVE SELF-TALK.

On a similar note, having negative thoughts about other people rattling around inside of you can be destructive. Don't spend your precious time stewing about someone else. You pay the price for your anger or jealousy (pick your emotion), not the other guy. He is doing fine. You, on the other hand, are carrying an extra burden. Throw it off. Free yourself from unnecessary negativity. Make it a habit. It will make you feel good.

14 DON'T BE A COMPLEXIFIER

What's the simplest way to make change for a dollar?
Most people will say four quarters. Why? Because it's much quicker and simpler than dealing with dimes, nickels and pennies. Sometimes it's best to do things the easy way.

> There is no reason to make simple things unnecessarily complex. Don't make easy matters hard.

If you want to practice being heliotropic, keep it simple. Do it in whatever way you can, however you can, to whomever you can. Avoid overthinking. Smile. Say hello. Hold the door open for someone. Give up your seat. Wish someone well. It takes very little effort to make people feel good.

Don't tax your brain. Think in terms of the four-quarter solution. Simple is best.

KEEP IT SIMPLE.

15 MAKE YOUR WORDS COUNT

When someone asks for a glass of water, don't hose them down. In one of the first public speaking classes I ever took, the instructor put a huge sign in the back of the room for us to see while giving our speeches.

In big bold letters the sign asked:

What's your point?

It's a good question to keep in mind at all times. People invariably get lost in too many words telling stories that go on and on and on and on without being aware of the reaction of the listener.

I suggest that you give people what they need without overwhelming them. Say what needs to be said and then be done. If people want more, let them ask for more. When they do, you know for sure that they are engaged.

SAY WHAT NEEDS TO BE SAID AND THEN BE DONE.

If you notice people becoming bored while you're talking, it's probably because you're boring them. Salt on the roots. Pay attention to how people are reacting. Think before you speak.

If there is not a moral or point to a story, if it's not somehow relevant to the listener, don't bother telling it in the first place. If you decide to tell your story, be brief. Say more with fewer words. It's difficult, but a great thing to practice.

Many people we know are truly wonderful, but they talk too much! (I could say more, but really, do I need to?)

DO THE

NEXT

RIGHT

THING

16 SPEAK FLUENT GRATITUDE

The research is clear. Cultivating gratitude makes you and the people around you feel better.

It feels good to be around people who are grateful rather than those who act like they are entitled. It feels good to be around people who express their gratitude.

> *"Thank you, I really appreciate it."*

It feels good to be around people who see opportunities to be grateful for their circumstances, not just grateful for their stuff.

> *"I'm happy to be here."*

We are inspired when we are around people who see silver linings in dark clouds. All of us have moment-to-moment choices to complain about what we don't have or don't want or to accept and embrace what we have and make the best of it.

> IT FEELS GOOD TO BE AROUND PEOPLE
> WHO EXPRESS THEIR GRATITUDE.

We can reframe anything that first appears negative to us. Instead of saying, "I've got to..." say, "I get to..." From "I have to go to work" to "I get to go to work." From "I have to visit my kids or parents" to "I get to visit my kids or parents."

It sounds simple because it is. That's the beauty of moving from "got to" to "get to." It moves us from salt on our roots to sun on our leaves.

But what about those times when you face real hardship? Personal tragedy. Despair. My advice is to take a moment at a time. Remember the bright moments that come your way. Celebrate little victories. Small blessings can add up to a much more positive state of mind.

Practice cultivating gratitude in your own way. You don't have to write a gratitude journal or make a big deal about it, but cultivate gratitude while waiting in line, while walking the dog, while commuting to work or while just doing nothing.

17 HELP OTHERS KEEP PERSPECTIVE

Dear Mom and Dad,
We had a little fire here last week, but don't worry.
I escaped through the bedroom window.
The doctors said I'll be fine and that the baby is OK.
I'm staying with my boyfriend at his apartment until all
the bandages are off and I move in with a friend
I met online.

Love,
Cindy,

P.S. There was no fire, I'm NOT pregnant,
I don't have a boyfriend; I failed my chemistry test.
Doesn't sound so bad now, does it?

Whether you use humor, worst-case scenarios or other strategies, learning to keep things in perspective is an important skill to develop, which is why I encourage you to practice quietly seeing the bigger picture.

The ability to see the forest separate from the trees comes with age and experience for sure, but almost anyone at any age can give us perspective. Have you ever witnessed a young child

PRACTICE QUIETLY SEEING THE BIGGER PICTURE.

watching two adults get upset over nothing and ask, "Mommy, why are those people so mad?" Kids are brilliant at seeing the simple things that we cannot.

When you help others find perspective, you can be a breath of fresh air, especially if you take the time to evaluate their unique circumstance. If you succeed, you can help turn a dark situation completely around. How heliotropic is that?

Offering your perspective to others is not a matter of offering your opinion. (Since your life and ideals may not translate to theirs, giving your opinion may be pouring salt on their roots.) It's good to check to see if a person is open to what you have to say. If your intention is sincere, chances are you will be helpful.

18 Do the next right thing

You made a mistake. A real blunder. You said the wrong thing, you made the wrong move. What do you do?

The answer is simple.
You do the next right thing.

If you don't like the outcome of the action you took,
do the next right thing, now.

You were entirely inappropriate.
Do the next right thing, now.

Decide what kind of person you want to be and ask yourself what that person would do in your situation.

Because I appreciate wisdom, I practice thinking of myself as a wise person. I ask myself, *"What would a wise person do here now?"*

This is also a good time to talk about the notion of being in the present moment, something that can be difficult and effortless at the same time. Being present means being aware of what's going on inside and around you. You hear things, you think things, you feel things, you see things, you smell things.

Do the next right thing, now.

If you are in the present, you will be paying attention. If you have salted someone's roots, you will need to take special care to help them recover. The past is past. If you need to apologize, apologize well. If you do something that is not quite right, you will know it. You will also most likely know how to correct it. You will know exactly the next right thing to do.

19 MAKE YOUR MOTIVE CLEAR AND CLEAN

It is important to understand your motive for doing or saying something and then make it clear to others. In other words, make sure that you have no hidden agenda. Avoid passive-aggressive behavior. Say what you mean and mean what you say and don't say it mean. People smell dishonest intentions. When you are about to act, ask yourself: What is my intention?

> SAY WHAT YOU MEAN
> AND MEAN WHAT YOU SAY
> AND DON'T SAY IT MEAN.

Consider also, whether your motive is pure. For instance, if your motive is to make someone aware of an error in their work so they won't make the same mistake again, good. Then it is pure, and the person is likely to accept what you have to say.

If your motive is to make someone aware of the error but also make them feel a little shame, your motive is impure, and the person will be rightly defensive. They will likely bristle when you speak to them again — for good reason.

In general, when we trust that a person has good intentions, we cut them slack. If we think their intent is impure, we distrust everything that they say from that point on. As long as your intention is positive, you do not have to worry about a thing. Intent will always carry the day.

When you are explicit about your intentions, others will then hold you to it, which is a good thing.

The moment there is suspicion about a person's motives,
everything he does becomes tainted.
– Mahatma Gandhi

20 TAKE THE HIGH ROAD

We are faced with a million choices in our lives when it comes to interactions with other people. Especially when people irritate us. Whether we are heliotropic or not often depends on which road we take. It's your choice.

> You can be pissed and petty,
> or gracious and forgiving.

I was reading a newspaper column on ethics. A man wrote in to ask how he should word a letter he wanted to write. The story is that the man and his brother had been estranged for years. His brother's death announcement mentioned all the survivors, including a deceased dog, but there was no mention of him. Yet, he still wanted to write a letter of condolence to his sister-in-law.

> AVOID THE ANGRY/HURT/INSULTED
> VERSION OF ANYTHING.

Since being heliotropic means being uplifting and helpful to others, the answer is very simple.

"I'm so sorry for your loss; I just wanted to express my deepest condolences. Even though we haven't spoken in 20 years, I want you to know I'm saddened by my brother's death and can only imagine your pain."

Avoid the angry/hurt/insulted version of anything. Taking the high road is always best for you and those around you. Test it out in the laboratory of your own experience.

PET
PEEVES
BITE

21 RELEASE YOUR PET PEEVES

We all have pet peeves. It's an unfortunate truth, but we do.
If you want to be more heliotropic, get rid of them.
Release them into the wild, never to return.

The problem with keeping them around is that we feed them and groom them, in essence nursing our irritation. Remember, the more we practice something the more automatic it becomes.

> ## EVEN IF YOU LOVE YOUR PET PEEVES, SET THEM, AND YOURSELF, FREE.

We basically train our pet peeves to keep us in a state of annoyance and then begin to feel righteous about it.

"Don't you hate it when…"
"I can't stand it when they don't…"
"Why don't they…"
"I don't understand why they do that!"

Being irritated is a way of pouring salt on your own roots while turning yourself into someone bound to pour salt on someone else's roots. After all, an irritated person is no fun to be around.

In order to be heliotropic, we have to practice feeding the part of ourselves that does not let ourselves be made miserable by life's little hassles. Feeding your pet peeves does the opposite. Even if you love your pet peeves, set them, and yourself, free.

For every minute you remain angry, you give up 60 seconds of peace of mind.
– Ralph Waldo Emerson

22 SMILE AND MOVE ON

Which is better, chocolate or vanilla?

This is not a trick question. Anyone with half a brain knows that chocolate is better. Am I right or am I right?

Oh, you think that I am wrong, that vanilla is better, and that I am presumptuous to state my opinion so firmly?

My question to you is, why does it matter what I say or believe? If I make a silly statement, one that you don't agree with, is it worth arguing about?

Don't waste your time and energy arguing about stupid stuff. "By the way, Barry Sanders was the greatest running back of all time!" Arguing to get someone to change their preference is useless; don't do it!

Trying to get someone to see the world the way you see it is energy wasted; don't do it!

Insisting that you're right about a personal preference will get you nowhere; don't do it!

There is no such thing as a universally beloved movie. Piece of music. Color. Flavor. Or running back. If someone insists (literally or figuratively) that vanilla is better, and it annoys you, shut up and smile. For those who don't understand what this has to do with being heliotropic, I'll be more explicit. If you argue about silly things without knowing it's just for fun, it is salt on roots.

 Keep your cool

Practicing the skill of keeping our cool with little things makes it easier when bigger stuff happens.

Don't you love it when during a crisis someone knows what to do and how to keep calm and carry on? I can't help but admire people like the pilot who landed his plane on the Hudson River when his engines went out, saving the lives of hundreds of people.

Most crises are not the kind where a plane loses both its engines. Most problems are mild pain-in-the-butt type problems that people make big by freaking out. My advice is, don't.

> PRACTICING THE SKILL OF KEEPING OUR COOL WITH LITTLE THINGS MAKES IT EASIER WHEN BIGGER STUFF HAPPENS.

When a problem arises, you have a choice to just clean it up, or complain about it and turn it into something that it is not. I've shared the perspective that most crises are the "clean up in aisle three" kind. They are problems that require someone to clean up the mess, nothing more.

Anyone who ever had pets or kids knows that poop and barf are part of the "joys" of living. Unpleasant, but no big deal.

If you freak out about everything, you will feel like your life is out of control. Remain unruffled, and you will find yourself living a more peaceful existence.

Keep your cool. Let a small issue remain small. Just handle it.

24 REMEMBER WHO YOU ARE

One of the most powerful predictors of our behaviors comes from who we think we are, because our identity predicts our conduct. It's quite profound, actually.

I have a friend who is extremely heliotropic. He sees himself as a person whose purpose is to let his life-force shine through. Those are his words, not mine. How do you think people experience him? Almost everyone who meets him or knows him thinks he is truly a good person. If you see yourself as a certain type of person, you will try to act like that person would act. It's that simple.

> IF YOU SEE YOURSELF
> AS A HELIOTROPIC PERSON,
> THE REST IS EASY.

If you see yourself as a heliotropic person, the rest is easy. Ask yourself what a heliotropic person would do in any given situation, then do whatever you think the heliotropic version of yourself would do.

And do more of that.

25 DECIDE WHAT MATTERS MOST

This is good advice for newlyweds, young parents, young leaders, even grandparents. But it's also good to remind ourselves of it daily: Pick your battles. Some things may be worth fighting for, arguing about or even dying for. Most things are not.

Be the person who knows the difference.

Be the person who can tell what is serious and what is not.

Be a person with a long fuse who thinks things through.

If you know what truly matters most to you, you will know how to make better decisions.

Do you really need to micromanage employees or grown kids? Do you want to get tangled in the mire of neighborhood gossip? Do you really want to fight about the crumbs on the counter? Is it really up to you to nip that problem in the bud at this moment?

Ask yourself again and again, does this matter to me?
Is it better to walk away? Say nothing? Address it another day?

These questions are challenging to figure out. Take the time to do it anyway. Your personal and professional relationships are priceless; honor them.

> ASK YOURSELF AGAIN AND AGAIN,
> DOES THIS MATTER?

Change your opinions, keep your principles;
change your leaves, keep intact your roots.
– Victor Hugo

26 FILL IN THE POTHOLES

The Parable of the Pothole

One night a young man is walking down a rough street in a poor neighborhood. Because the street is badly maintained and dimly lit, he trips in a pothole. Picking himself up, hurt, bruised and angry, he asks, "Why me? And why don't people take care of things?"

Time passes. The man finds himself on that street quite often, but having fallen, he is wiser, more street-smart. He sees the pothole and walks around it, asking himself, "Why doesn't someone fix that?"

Time passes. Life has become good for the man. He doesn't have to spend time in that neighborhood or walk down that street anymore. He walks down different streets. Smooth, well-cared-for, easier streets. That old street is irrelevant to him now; he doesn't think about it.

Time passes. It's been years since the man has been on that old street. He reflects on his life and the many things he has attained. He also remembers falling into the pothole and recalls the injury he suffered. He goes back to the street and sees that the pothole is still there. No one has fixed it. He realizes that he can repair it. So he does.

YOU CAN MAKE A DIFFERENCE
IN OTHER PEOPLE'S LIVES
AT ANY TIME.

Doing good when you don't have to. Thinking about ways to help other people avoid making the mistakes that you made. These are ways to be heliotropic. You don't have to announce to the world what a great pot-hole filler you are. But if you can find ways to prevent others from getting hurt, why not? The good news is that you can make a difference in other people's lives at any time. Do it now. Even though you don't have to.

27 Do it anyway

All our excuses are legitimate. (He was rude.)
Be heliotropic anyway.

All of the reasons why it's hard to be heliotropic are true. (I was tired.)
Be heliotropic anyway.

All of the explanations for why you haven't been heliotropic are accurate. (It wasn't fair.)
Be heliotropic anyway.

Our do-it-anyway muscles are all different sizes. Some of us have highly developed muscles that allow us to push through our discomfort easily. Regardless of size, use whatever you have to do it anyway.

You will be better for it.

Your life will be better for it.

The lives of the people around you
will be better for it.

Yes, no matter what challenges lie ahead of you,
be heliotropic anyway.

> ### No matter what challenges lie ahead of you, be heliotropic anyway.

Knowing is not enough; we must apply.
Willing is not enough; we must do.
– Johann Wolfgang von Goethe

28 PRACTICE, PRACTICE, PRACTICE

It is a myth that practice makes perfect. It doesn't. What you practice makes you better at what you practice. There is no perfect. I heard a story that illustrates this idea.

The Parable of the Two Wolves

One evening, a wise old man told his grandson about a battle that goes on inside people. He said, "My son, the battle is between two wolves inside us all. One is Evil — it is anger, envy, jealousy, greed and arrogance. The other is Good — it is peace, love, hope, humility, compassion and faith."

The grandson thought about this for a while and then asked his grandfather, "Which wolf wins?" The old man replied, "The one you feed."

People who are wise already know this. What the old man didn't tell his grandson is that the battle rages daily, moment to moment. If you practice irritation, judgment and anger, those qualities get stronger as sure as night follows day.

Good and evil, kindness and cruelty, wisdom and ignorance. Choose sides. Put on your uniform. And get in the game.

> YOU GET A CHANCE TO TRY AGAIN
> EVERY MOMENT OF EVERY DAY
> OF EVERY YEAR OF YOUR LIFE.

Just remember, practice increases your chances of winning. And here's the best part. If you lose the game today, you get to play again. If you want to be heliotropic, practice. Just as the sun rises to create a new day every 24 hours, you get a chance to try again every moment of every day of every year of your life.

29 BE AN OLYMPIC LISTENER

I advised a client to strive to become an Olympic listener.
He got it. He knows like all of us that everything speaks if we are paying attention. The challenge is to develop and practice the art of listening to what is said, what is not said, and, most of all, what is meant.

Another executive said when she learned to listen more deeply, she became more sensitive to things that were unspoken as well as those that were spoken. As she began to observe more closely and become a more careful listener, she found that she could discern what people really needed.

That is part of what being the sun is about. Giving people what they need. It's also knowing that what is sun to some people, may be salt to others.

> EVERYTHING SPEAKS
> IF WE ARE PAYING ATTENTION.

Here are some listening tips:

Look people in the eye.

Put away your cell phone.

Put away your cell phone. (*Worth repeating.*)

Speak less than you think you should.

Ask short questions.

Try to learn something.

Be curious.

Be respectful.

Smile.

Don't interrupt.

Don't talk about yourself.

Don't look elsewhere while listening.

Don't prepare your remarks while listening.

Don't lose your temper.

If you practice Olympic listening, you will never lose.

30 Frickin' do it

The two most important words in this little book are: *Do it.*
I added frickin' to give the phrase some oomph, but truthfully,
do it are powerful words all on their own. *Do it* is the whole
enchilada. Because knowing isn't doing and it's the doing that
makes the difference.

My hope is that this book — the ideas and explanations it
contains — will work to remind you to think, speak and act in
ways that help yourself and others in some way.

If you already intentionally practice being heliotropic in all the
ways you can, fantastic. Please don't stop. *Do it* more. I am
grateful to you. You are making the world a better place.
If any of this information, or knowledge or wisdom nudges
you toward action that truly helps you and someone else,
hallelujah! We did some good.

> I wish you well and encourage you to
> Be the Sun, Not the Salt.

Peace,
Harry

IT'S THE DOING THAT
MAKES THE DIFFERENCE.

www.bethesunnotthesalt.com